Holiday Treats

Martha Mier

Foreword

Piano teachers are always searching for holiday solos to help their students celebrate those special days throughout the year. *Holiday Treats*, Book One will provide teachers and students with holiday solos for an entire year, all under one cover.

The music in this collection was written especially for the first year piano student, with solos in Middle C position. Optional teacher/parent duets are provided for some of the solos for a fuller sound and to encourage rhythmic security.

I hope students will love sharing this special music with family and friends throughout the year.

Happy Holidays!

Contents

Halloween:
Happy Halloween 2

Thanksgiving:
A Special Day 4

Hanukkah:
Happy Hanukkah! 6

Christmas:
Christmas Is Coming! 8

Valentine's Day:
My Valentine Friend 10

St. Patrick's Day:
Leprechaun Parade 12

Easter:
The Happy Bunny 14

Fourth of July, Canada Day, Australia Day:
Celebration Day 16

Copyright © MCMXCII by Alfred Publishing Co., Inc.
Art Direction: Ted Engelbart
Cover Design: Trish Meyer
All rights reserved.   Printed in USA.

Happy Halloween

Happily

Martha Mier

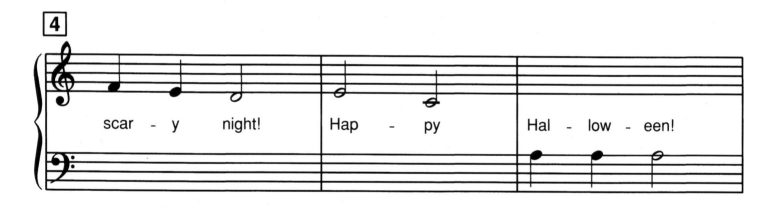

DUET PART (Student plays 1 octave higher.)

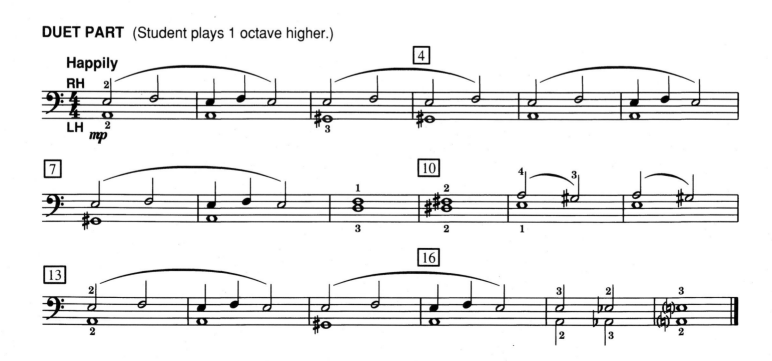

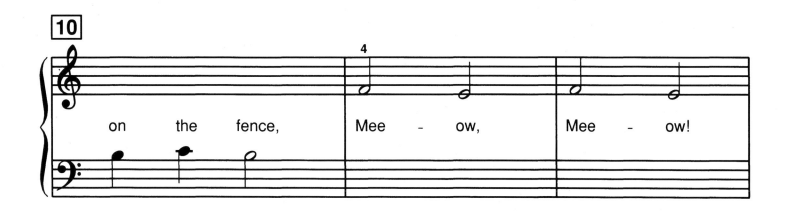
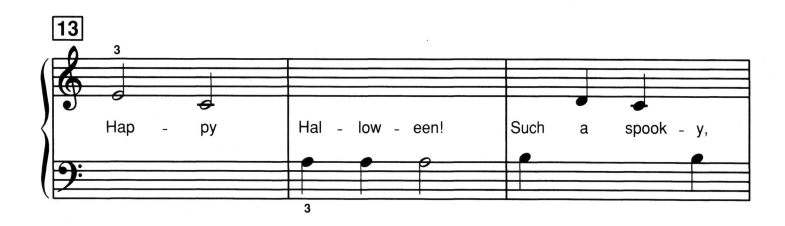
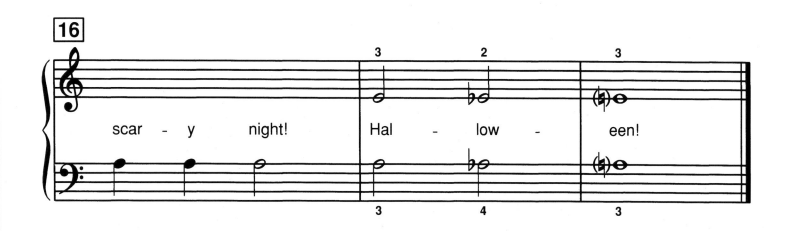

A Special Day

Moderately slow

Martha Mier

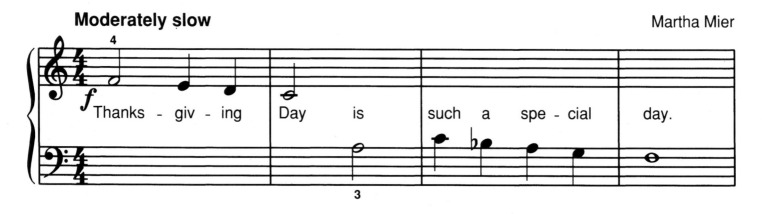

Thanks - giv - ing Day is such a spe - cial day.

DUET PART (Student plays 1 octave higher.)

Moderately slow

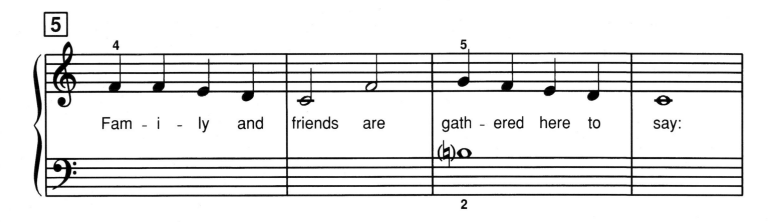
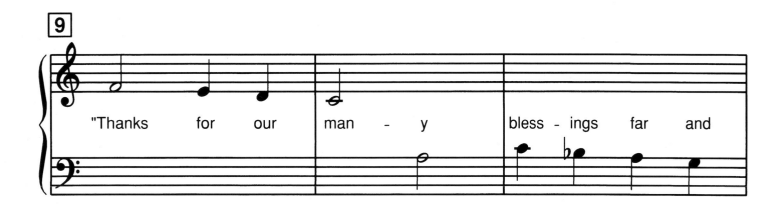
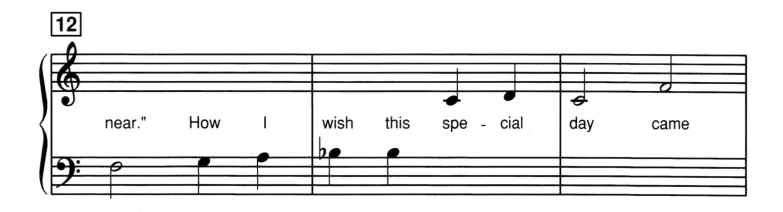
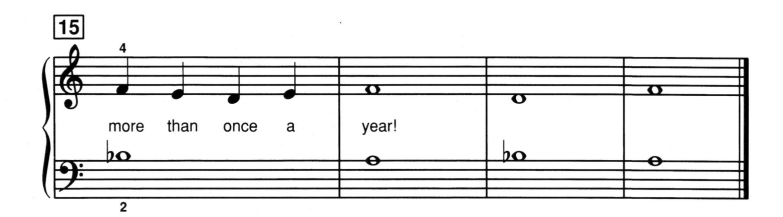

Happy Hanukkah!

Martha Mier

Happily

Hap - py, hap - py Ha - nuk - kah, fes - ti - val of

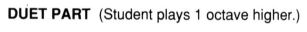

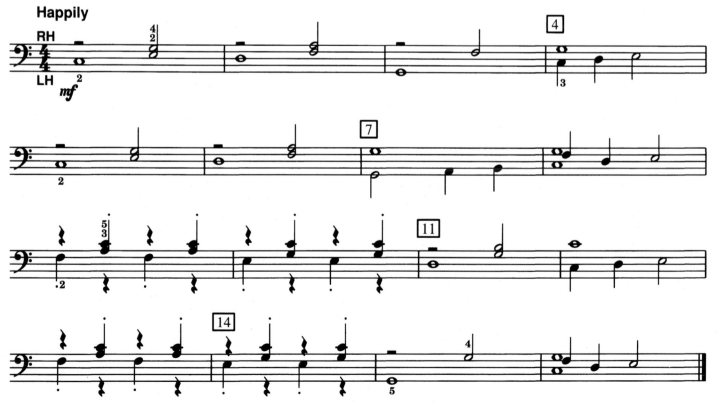

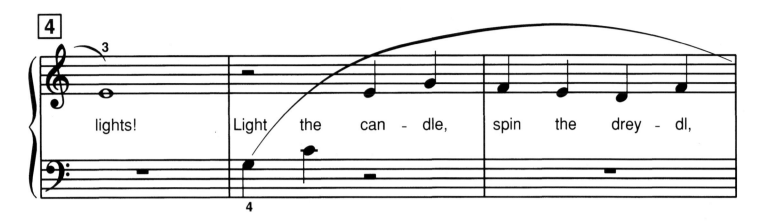
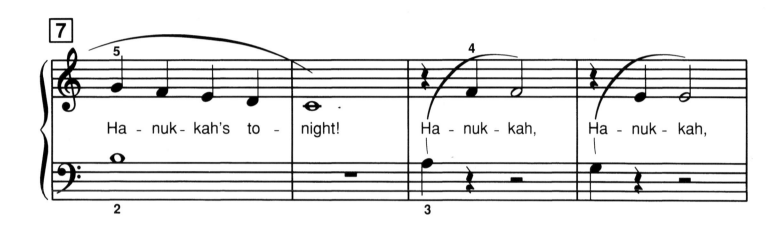
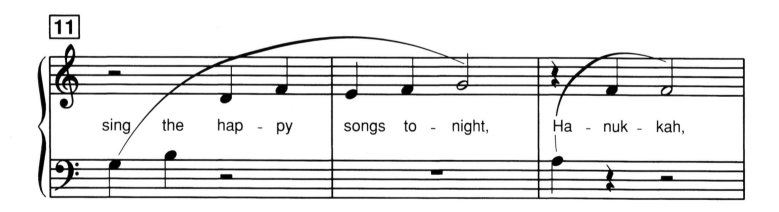
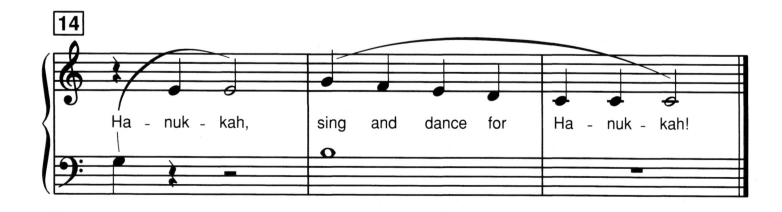

Christmas is Coming

Martha Mier

DUET PART (Student plays 1 octave higher.)

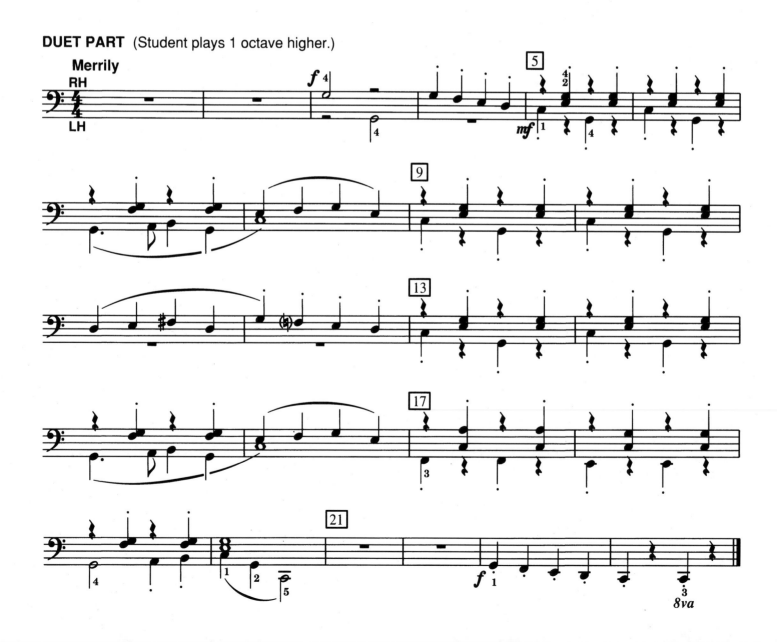

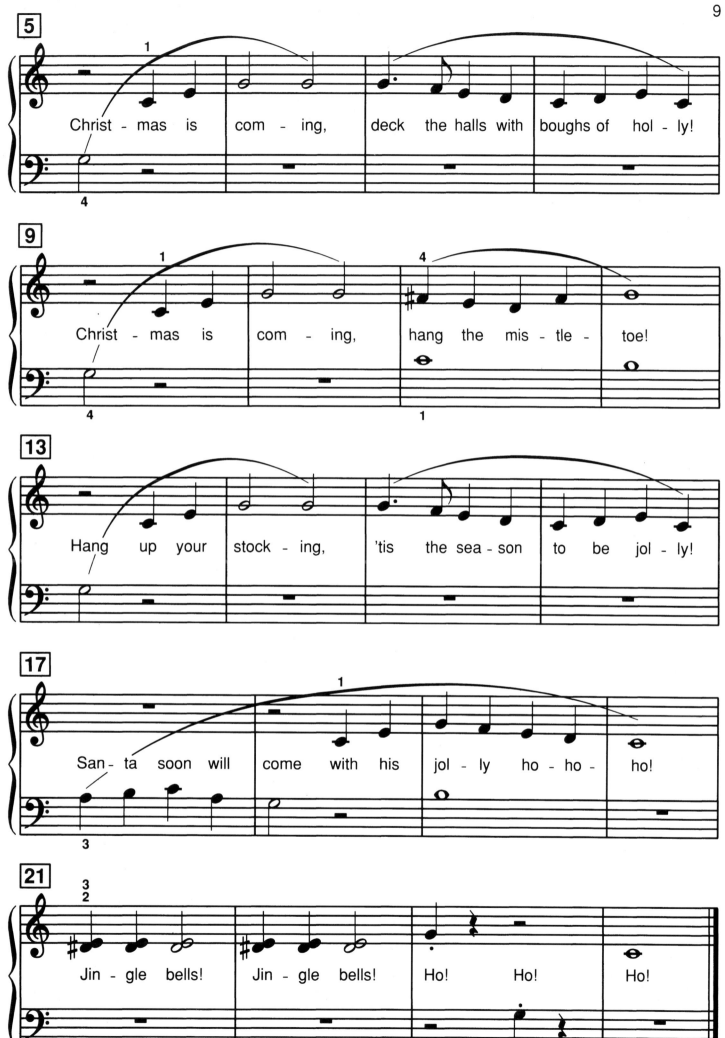

My Valentine Friend

Martha Mier

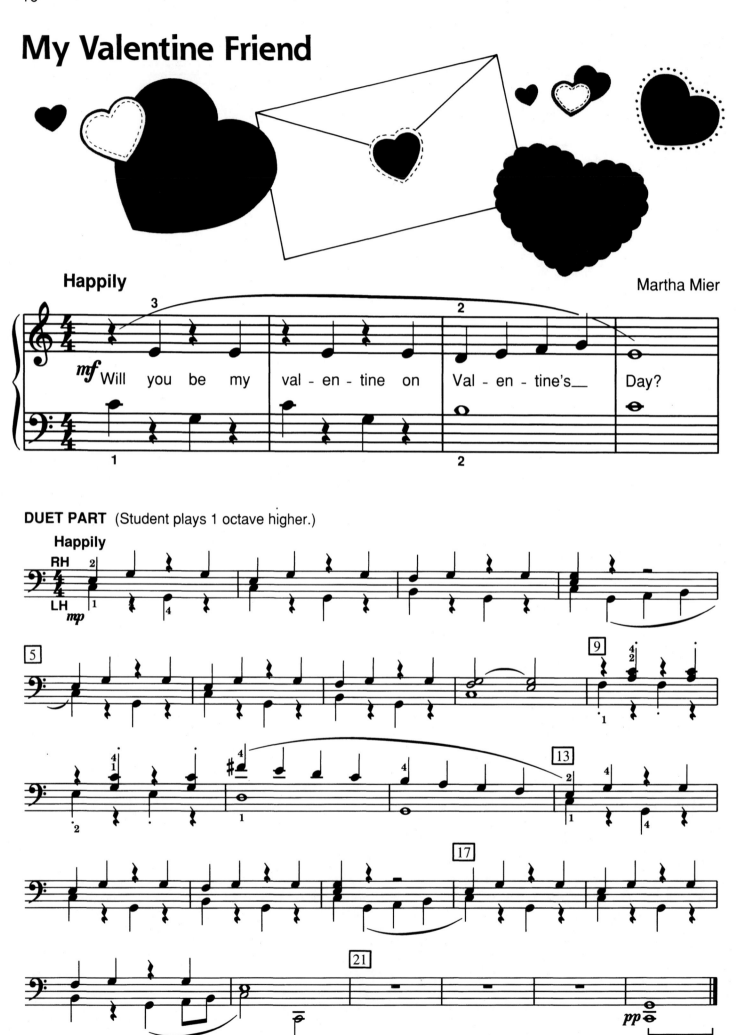

Leprechaun Parade

Martha Mier

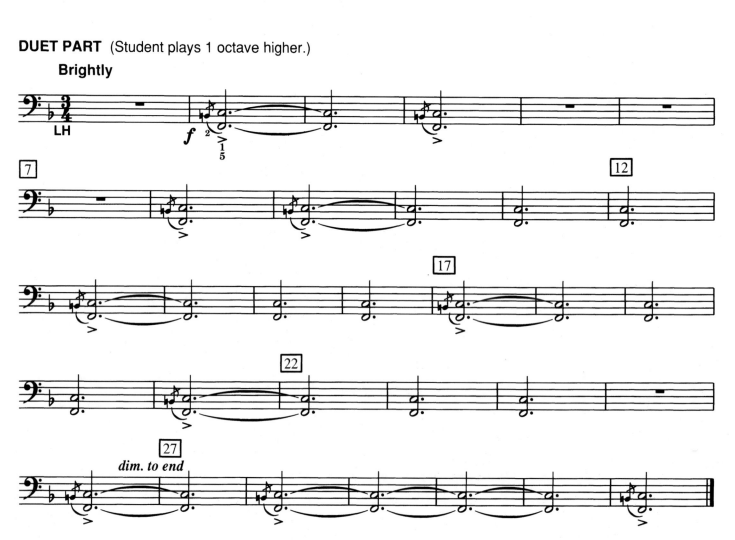

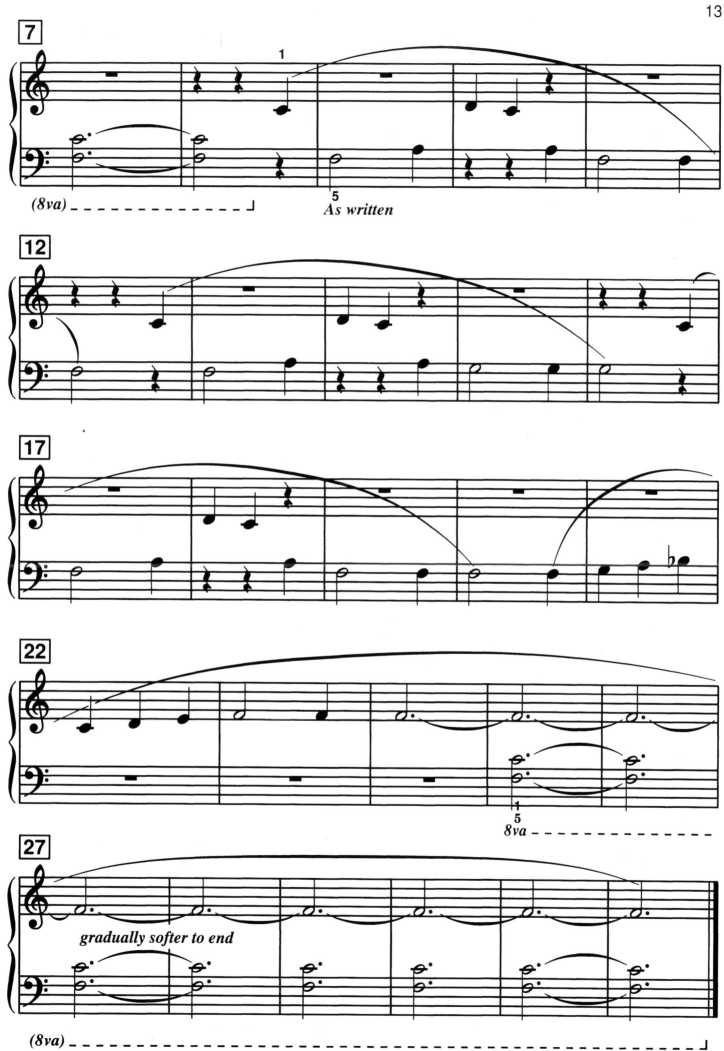

The Happy Bunny

Happily

Martha Mier

Did you see the East-er Bun-ny hop right past here,

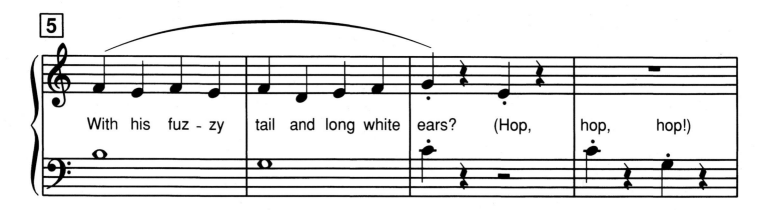

With his fuz-zy tail and long white ears? (Hop, hop, hop!)

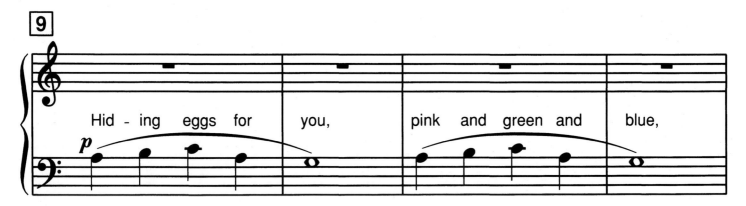

Hid-ing eggs for you, pink and green and blue,

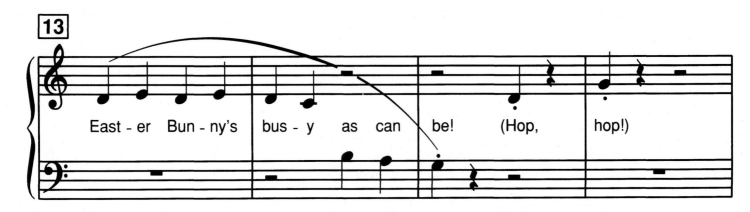

East-er Bun-ny's bus-y as can be! (Hop, hop!)

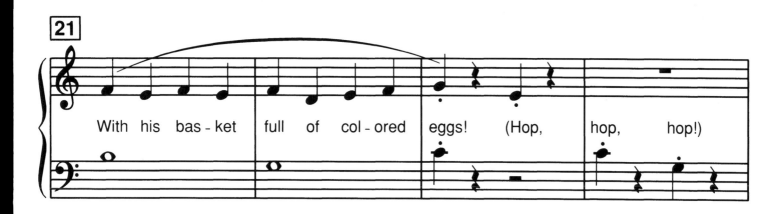
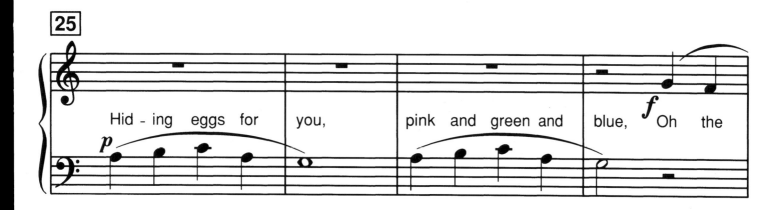
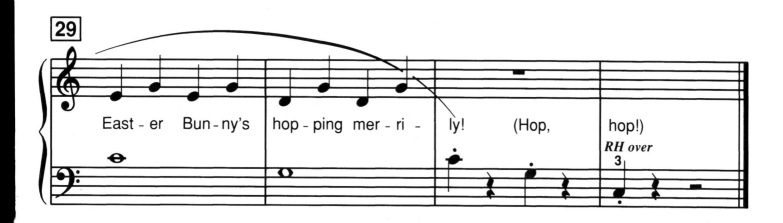